KEENER SOUNDS

A SUITE

Also by Roger Greenwald

Poetry

Connecting Flight

Slow Mountain Train

The Half-Life

An Opening in the Vertical World

Poetry in Translation

The Silence Afterwards: Selected Poems of Rolf Jacobsen

Stone Fences, by Paal-Helge Haugen (trans. with William Mishler)

The Time in Malmö on the Earth, by Jacques Werup

Wintering with the Light, by Paal-Helge Haugen

Did I Know You? Thirty-one poems by Rolf Jacobsen

Through Naked Branches: Selected Poems of Tarjei Vesaas

North in the World: Selected Poems of Rolf Jacobsen

Picture World, by Niels Frank

Meditations on Georges de La Tour, by Paal-Helge Haugen

Guarding the Air: Selected Poems of Gunnar Harding

Through Naked Branches: Selected Poems of Tarjei Vesaas, Revised Edition

Fiction in Translation

A Story about Mr. Silberstein, by Erland Josephson

I Miss You, I Miss You! by Peter Pohl and Kinna Gieth

ROGER GREENWALD

Keener Sounds
A Suite

With paintings by Arielle Sandler

BLACK WIDOW PRESS

Boston, MA

Black Widow Press is an imprint of Commonwealth Books, Inc., Boston, MA. Distributed to the trade by NBN (National Book Network) throughout North America, Canada, and the U.K. All Black Widow Press books are printed on acid-free paper and glued into bindings. Black Widow Press and its logo are registered trademarks of Commonwealth Books, Inc.

Joseph S. Phillips and Susan J. Wood, Ph.D., Publishers
www.blackwidowpress.com

ISBN-13: 979-8-9911391-1-3
Library of Congress Control Number: 2025931952

This book has been composed in Minion Pro.
The paper used in this publication meets the minimum requirements of ANSI/NISO Z39.48–1992 (R 1997) (Permanence of Paper).

Printed in Canada

10 9 8 7 6 5 4 3 2 1

For Christiane Lieberman

Contents

KEENER SOUNDS

A SUITE

Oh! Blessed rage for order, pale Ramon,
The maker's rage to order words of the sea,
Words of the fragrant portals, dimly-starred,
And of ourselves and of our origins,
In ghostlier demarcations, keener sounds.

— Wallace Stevens

Aubade

Who sees the dark between the laughing flames?
Who measures blackness beneath the sun?
Who guesses there are minutes dense as clay?
Who eats regret for what can't be undone?

Who sizes up a vacuum at a glance?
Who found that one and one and one make one?
Who etches sorrow as its own last dance
and dances solo when honeysuckles hum?

Who wishes Handan happiness, although
his wishing hasn't yielded him a fig?
Who felt without connection nothing grows
and watched its death blight every living thing?

Who sings a song of questions full of snow?
Who smiles if just one reader thinks she knows?

I *Prélude*

Auditorium

I couldn't see you. Garish lighting draped
your face in shadow: circled eyes, darkened
lips, even your hair a stranded map
of bright rivers and black roads, with no legend.

I couldn't hear you. Vivaldi sang to God
through you, but you were ancillary, dancers
gauzed in white were center stage, a mob
of pulsing angels who circled, reveled, pranced.

Their bare arms grazed in curving strokes, they stretched
their hands above their heads as if in praise
of spotlight spirits, Terpsichore in the wings.

Yet this body too could serve its wish:
while others sat entranced and fixed their gaze
on motion, I closed my eyes to hear you sing.

for Suzie LeBlanc

Annbjørg Lien

Each string a path to hillside, forest, rose.
And she can take a couple at a time,
make of ancient modes a modern rhyme
that echoes by her cheekbone as she bows.

As deep as songs with lyrics hope to be,
how can dance become a song that's deeper?
How can the mute and numbly rambling sleeper
wake with dream intact in a ringing tree?

Wooded silence lives in inlaid wood,
preserved, contained—and then released, renewed.
It blossoms when Hardanger strings are trued
and Lien's fingers make the promise good.

Through shaded time and brightest nerve she bows;
The hillside is her name—and she, the Rose.

[AHN-byeurg LEE-en: *eu* as in French *acteur*]

Bridal March

When Susanne Lundeng plays the Bridal March
from Beiarn, bride and groom and all their train
make their stately way across terrain
shaped by glaciers, up the hills to church

and down again on stone-built paths and flowering
slopes in seven shades of green. Now solemn
their embrace, now spirited the column
of dancing friends and kin, the fiddlers bowing

in unison the weave of generation:
repeated recombining of shifted notes
ranged on spindled threads, a theme to play on.

The distant guests return along the coast;
their faces echo all our celebrations
when Susanne gives the Bridal March from Beiarn.

[su-SAH-neh LUNN-deng: *U* as in *pull*]
[BAYE-ahrn: *AYE* as in *aye-aye*]

Ethos and Mythos

Dusty marriage manuals happened on
in antiquarian booksellers' cluttered stalls
anatomize how spouses are enthralled
as spirits meld in overlapping zones.

A novel too, if French and old enough,
may dare to conjure up the body's rapture
and through an earthy lyricism capture
sensual creatures' leap to physical love.

How quaint and stale and tragically unhip,
sublime, deluded, phallocentric, dull,
the remnants of a male Romantic cult
whose centuries seem a historical blip.

Yet in their chambers lovers still look back—
and flee from Hades, singing of their luck.

Happiness

Happiness was washing clothing hauled
by bus with beat-up suitcase, ancient canvas
knapsack, in the town's one coin laundry
half an hour away at Danmarks Plass.

I wore a woolen cap and borrowed topcoat,
she her grandpa's leather jacket, cracked
and smoothly worn as cobblestones, too short
to hide the *busserull's* buckle at the back.

You fold the linens lengthwise, then tug,
trust your weight to stretching sheets, to woman
on the other end, your smiling love.
It never failed: mundane, exalted, human.

Those who call this mere domesticity
would scorn the sunlight as quotidian.

[BUSS-eh-rull: both *u*'s as in *pull*] laborer's shirt

II Allemande

Halfway There

The sky pressed down, a potlid of aluminum,
matte-gray, scarred and pitted, battered, dented;
somewhere was a valve, its narrow lumen
a possible way out, if fate relented.
Somewhere a place for us, the West-side tune,
extending Ludwig's, floated plaintively.
The prior problem—boarding the balloon—
can't vie with star-crossed lovers' reveries.

Which time and place might yield an us, the song
did not reveal. Meanwhile, my father's loss
made loss my mother's mate, made her long
for company under the lowering sky.
I flew, I crossed an ocean, found the place.
But when my love stole time, there was no why.

Remembrance

My calling was recalling. It was my move
to conjure the father I hadn't known. Or at least
hold loss's grief, behind which lay the love
I'd felt. Like drinking beer to get the yeast.

Drunk on grief, I insisted I was sober;
not solemn, but a more than serious boy.
Alone, I learned the art of crossing over
to the lazy crescent river, early day.

And then the shaking nights till love returned.
And later, choking nights when love betrayed.
And then the fantasy that what had burned
might live again if raked with words. This way.

Oh! Cursèd rage for memory, pallid lover,
who turned to ash, vanished over the water.

Numbers

He died at twenty-nine, his son was two.
You left when I was thirty-three; we had,
as lawyers write sans irony, no issue.
But *men* don't need to watch a clock, you said.

His radar reached the moon, but his PhD
remained unfinished: Theory of Numbers. Now
I wrote my own, six hundred pages in three
short stints. In weeks you tired anyhow,

threw years away, the past and future: laughter,
language, mountains, music, children—loving.
"Yeah, I know, *he* had one, so *you* have to."
"He wasn't done." You winced but realized nothing.

I'd told you of my father. You forgot it.
I would have died for you. You never got it.

Phoenix

Now my mother's dying and you're not here
—again. As when her father died in Phoenix.
His final blessing: *Gey gezunterheyt.*
We kissed, his stubble printing on my skin.

How were things between us, was his question.
Little did I know ... that as I grieved,
you snuck off to rent your one-room bastion,
lay there half in love with deadly ease.

How is it that your absence is still absence
twenty-five years on, your smell so near
it might as well be ink from rotary presses,
vapor off rustling newsprint I still hear.

Was *Forverts* written backwards—or *English* type?
What's true—love's memory, or "liberation's" hype.

Collisions

When I think about my life from after it
a dark determination colors it,
as if the death of a young physicist
unbound cascades whose traces hobbled it.

How could my mother's verve have vanquished that—
the swerving fragments flew and that was that.
Remarriage can't restore the atom smashed,
nor backward glance revive Schrödinger's cat.

As for G., her father's drink was death,
and here came I, looking to connect.
I didn't know she wore this fatal wreath:
resentment's orbiting clouds bedecked her head.

So, grief transformed, you love, the gift received.
Yet firmest bond is split when half's aggrieved.

Safety

Fear on waking: she said the chiffonier
in our bedroom was a mastodon.
A metaphor—looming. I didn't hear
what lay ahead: how any sudden hand

gesture in my talk would make her shrink.
Here was fear I couldn't fathom, severe,
deep-rooted, unabating. A sinkhole
was swallowing the safety we had savored.

Then a day when she answered spectral dialogue.
"What do you think I said?" She quoted. "No,
I haven't said a thing." Reply: "You're lying."
A stopping place with nowhere left to go.

Through curved windows dark filled the living space.
In dim silence, our history displaced.

Night

Don't I want to sleep at night, or is it
that living dayside spooks me half to death?
Sun-up flares an arc of daunting length;
I keep it out, brightness invisible.

Daylight's for action, action needs forgetting:
ancient conversations yield no gains.
Night's the time for those who hear refrains;
morning dreams, not mornings, their regrets.

Mask of dusk, the planet's shadow, rises.
Day's lacunae fade, and though night's bare,
remembered voices scarcely interfere
with unforgotten body, those clear eyes.

Draw the curtains, lower blinds, turn off
the phone. Not even night is night enough.

Nausea

Why does nausea rise when nighttime thickens
or more precisely, in the smallest hour,
famously dark? Call it mourning sickness,
a childless grief that overcomes the father

who never was. The man who hasn't known
small grip, hungry wail, the newborn's smell,
the questing gaze of blue eyes half his own,
the frighteningly mortal fontanelle;

first solid food, first step, first word, first fall,
the questions what and how and why and why,
first book, pen, drum, paint, joke, fight, school-day, mall,
fevers, music, parties, tears and sighs.

At night these shapes of absence fill his throat
and retching waves of nothing vomit out.

The Word *Wife*

—which so appalls young Singh in *The Mimic Men*
stalls my own brain differently. As when
a student said his wife agreed I'd marked him
too low. You have a *wife* and you *complain?*
I thought—and struggled not to say it. Lately
each occurrence sends my mind away,
and as the speaker glides I concentrate
to hear him, but end up mainly where I stray.

Absence from The Nights of Summer. Here's
The Specter of the Rose; the loveless life
of leaving coasts where ocean shrouds the ears.
And at my bitter mouth a married eye:
when Í say, Lucky man who has a wife,
shé says, Oh, what happened—did she die?

Mettle

And if I held the dead so close, how could I
ever let the living go? So precious
to me, this intertwining life, a mesh of
cognate language, skin and mind. Why would I?
This moving on they speak of—where's the draw?
You rip the web, you leave behind a wreck
of severed nerves that cannot re-connect.
No dagger ever leaves a wound as raw.

Of course I see this loyalty betrays me,
fierce commitment renders me unfit,
dwelling on remembered feeling grays me.
So I've revived myself with quickened wit,
am ready to embrace whoever sways me.
If she can grasp the silver of the love bit.

III Courante

Sightseeing

This is the harbor. Trondheim, 1 p.m.
The forecast's right: today is partly fine.
The boat to Munkholmen departs on time,
but what's the age of this fair deckhand, when

did she start working here, and how can they
go on with ropes and motor, orders called?
She can't be mortal if human genes are flawed;
the monks at least would know to stop and pray.

Ten minutes out; the docking takes as long.
Her sneakered feet, her hands on braided line—
she jumps ashore, but just before she lands,
I press the camera. Hopeless. Out of time.

She never looks. I note the tower's round.
It's called sightseeing. But Munkholmen's gone.

If I Told You

If I told you I was in a galaxy
of tall, curvy women with perfect skin,
that the warmth of their bodies varied directly
as the square of their distance, and amid this freezing engine

of desire I felt none, but only the suck
of absent desire, the longing waste of it,
like a gray monk's hunger for a red pulp
of fruit he isn't sure he's ever tasted;

if I told you these women always paid me
attention of a fleeting sort, their eyes
like those of comets whose tails stretch away
as they approach a stream of glancing ions,

would you call it dream-talk, nightmare's shocking moan—
or God's own rack and pinion: downtown Stockholm.

Eclipse

The sun rose in a cloud and people asked
Who are you, and Do you have the time
exactly? Doubled film and welder's glass
shielded their eyes, rigged up in every kind

of mask, a Halloween begun at dawn.
We'd hurried here—walked, biked, driven—and now
we waited, anxious, pulled by mystery known
for ages, seeking dark blessing: Show how

to find a mate I feel I've met before,
conjoining parts a perfect fit like these.
But afterwards we switch to *why:* Why tease

by keeping knowledge out of view? And sure
as this yields silence, ask ourselves advice:
How live when heaven's shadow rides my life?

Flora and Fauna

There's a bird that sounds like a squeaky bicycle chain
and a flower that smells like air from a rubber tire.
I looked for the sound where a sandaled foot was power
and for the smell where cars ramped up into rain.

But the sound wasn't perched below the shapely rear,
the fragrance didn't drift with a passing driver:
the bird was in a tree I couldn't discover,
the blossom on a branch behind my ear.

What's the point of tracking sensory clues,
a habit evolved to catch prey and not become it?
City's not savanna; I seek the summit
where you're a You to me, and I to you.

Though I wrote this as a change from my usual plaint,
it's not about its title, so it ain't.

Sunny Sweden

Pretend the women are holographic ads
since you've long been numb to ads' invasion
of deepest needs, have practiced hard
to stay aloof from images' persuasion.

How else survive the simplest stroll along
the walking-street, river of lustrous tans,
full figures, hair that smells of sun;
clean sweat, cotton colors, long-fingered hands.

Can't talk to ads. But if these shapes are flesh
you might as well drink up at the Irish pub
The Loft on Government Street, jump off the bridge
between the stony-headed lions, rub

shoulders with the pavement's softened tar,
and at last make contact with people driving cars.

Old with Wandering

I've crossed an ocean, bringing painted silk;
she plays below an open shell, as rain
trades parts with slanting light above our hill
and I shelter under shed-eaves with another man.

Shining moment! when, her niece in arms,
delight connects our eyes, the gap is closed,
I give her flowers and "Open this at home,"
our foreheads touch, her people stare, time slows.

With ringing ears, blood serene, I wait.
She calls, she's torn, her boy, she says, is back
tomorrow and she loves him so! "Dear heart,
go." In the dusk at Hotel Book I shake—

and weep—and thank the God I don't believe
for making me this gift I cannot have.

IV Sarabande

The Deep Heart's Core

My mother lived by sevens: seven years
in love with her young physicist before
they married, seven after—eyes as clear
in baby pics as lakes in fairy stories.

Acute leukemia ended this, brought seven
years of widowhood. Her second best
lasted seven too: the med-school-heaved
accountant, stopped by cardiac arrest.

Then the scheme breaks down. Quite soon a third:
danced with a wealthy merchant twenty years,
till death cut in. Yet sevens were a base.

"Lewis's writing," she whispers, photo turned.
"After him, how could you not compare?"
She says: "I put that in a secret place."

Cancer

The cancer's made her slim as a high school senior—
the senior she was when elders were still called *old.*
She'd fit her graduation photo's sailor
dress—though *journey*'s a gloss she can't be sold.

Her sepia smile is shy and innocent;
the Great Depression's scars will tighten later—
contracture not described by medicine
although her cohort shows a fearsome rate.

Sweet-hearted Mother, greeting Death five times—
five times! not counting parents... Couldn't It
have spared you this one, let you sail in time
without end, at least a hundred? Couldn't It?

You say don't cry for you, but I can't lie:
Tears are the human thing that will not die.

Silence and Semaphore

Home was noise, a clattered spoon, my mother's
piercing voice. And how I relished, first
night in my own apartment, breathing utter
quiet! But as she whispers to her nurse

I think, *Speak up!* (I'll keep my secrets; don't
keep yours.) Her sentences efficient, terse
as two-year-olds'—without delighted points.
Not *Truck! Giraffe!* but *Bathroom. Soda. Worse.*

Pointing means *I want,* a semaphore
of need. Her mind's all there, it's just that innards
often snag her thoughts, leave no more
than energy for basics: time and words

both short. Now silence is a shocking pall.
And my house too is missing new life's squall.

Farewells

When I, bereft, abandoned, went to ground,
grieving for the kids I'd never have,
"Next time pick someone who will stay around,"
my mother, twice a widow, said. A stab.
"Next time pick someone who will stay alive!"
I nearly parried. Didn't. But when she lay,
a widow yet again, about to die,
I left, to spare myself. Cruelty repaid?

Before that flight, I slept between her walls
through weeks of wasting, music, shunning touch.
Her body folding, I asked if she recalled
a phrase I'd taught her—I had a hunch on which.
She brightened. But *Kjære mor* wasn't what had held.
Tusen takk! she whispered—Thanks so much!

[approx. SHAR-eh MOOR: *A* as in *Sharon*] Dear Mother

Red and White

Grandpa was White Russian, but a Red for all that.
Did I tell him of Color War at summer camp?
My father's white cells won—too young, like him.
For Grandpa, later, red ones failed: default.

In childhood fevers, Whites were evil sailors
fought by other Whites: horse, hat, lance, knight.
In teen years whites were tennis players' outfits
and white balls flew in aces, slices, rallies.

I didn't know white nights were bright, not snowy,
I slid on Dostoevsky as on black ice:
"My God, a single moment of happiness—
enough for a lifetime." Would that be my story?

I've seen the midnight sun. That ought to last.
As what? A phrase, a slide. The moment passed.

Widows and Orphans

A Brit whose husband died in Afghanistan,
who shamed the PM to get better gear
for those still there, confirms, in this third year,
that her (not "our") seven-year-old son
is fine; and yes, she says, she's moving on,
she's with a man who serves, so knows the scene.
The interviewer lost his wife; he's been
through this, he claims, and asks her how it's gone.

My mother managed it. But I aspired
to stay who I was. As Stepman planned a claim,
a forced adoption, I prepared to hire
lawyers. A patent of no special fame
and I, RG, were all my father sired.
No fucking way would I erase his name.

New Year's Eve

This serial divorce, in which time leaves
the year embraced through fifty-two weeks
for a younger year, the old one left to grieve.
The marriage drops the ball. Sorrow wakes.

Mommy out, I spent the night with Nana
and Grandpa Charlie. Bright apartment—glassware
in heirloom cabinet; Depression-era
paintings; on black-and-white TV: Times Square.

These lovely people whom I loved—Marie
with shining lenses wire-framed, and Charles K.
in vest and tie, teaching me gin-rummy—
had lost their son. Did it feel that way?

This night when all the missing ones are missed.
The count of years without the midnight kiss.

Legacy

Flat roof of New York building, ’30s snapshot:
sun-softened, asphalt-smelling, snakes of glistening
tar on seams; crowd of immigrant sisters,
brothers, cousins. Mother’s people, up top.

Father’s father, in jacket, vest and tie,
brown shiny shoes (round toes, stiff leather soles),
sixty years past Cooper Union and girls
in Greenwich Village when 1900 arrived,

manned a bench outside my junior high.
It all ends here, a park in Copenhagen,
where sensual women stroll in the King’s Garden
with men engaged in their familiar lives:

“Anna, could you hold this for a minute?”
I hold my own, use my knees to clamp it.

Sunday Nights

Through the 50s, cities flickered blue
on Sunday nights: TVs' frosted fires
drew silent families close in solitudes
soon mapped from space by charge-coupled devices.

In that Sunday darkness teens could only sigh;
then decades of laissez-faire and vain divorce
made adults hooked on work and SSRIs
eager to save their necks in Monday's noose.

Sunday night! That dusk still chokes me, cafés
wind down, stragglers clasp cups, search dregs, resist
the advances of the wall clock, its monotone hum:

Go home it's done return another day.
Sunday night it's night worldwide, as if
the sun were gone on the day named for the sun.

V *Gavotte*

Uncertainty Principle

Is sex a theater of affections, or more
like reciprocating use, an engine geared
to satisfy each urge? You interfere
by asking, observer charges can't ignore.

The acts won't yield an answer, least of all
when one (just one) desires to be used
and wants not playful gift but *drive* to use—
Could a flavor, tasted, later come to gall?

Trust's the issue—and whether it will hold,
a doubt that, craving love, discolors lust,
beforehand spins to rest entangled thrust.
What's spooky—leaps to faith, or breaks foretold?

Bad timing's scarily good at prophecy.
And circling questions scatter blank debris.

Bitter Mint

Stopped yelling at myself as soon as you said
it troubled you. I'd thought that blowing steam
that way was harmless. For I'd kept my pledge
and rarely spoken harshly to you. Just to me.

"Idiot! Why can't you find that check?
I'm so fed up with this perpetual mess!
You know it was right here last time you looked!
You're wasting time you can't afford to waste!"

You sat there one floor down with your computer,
silent, gleaning evidence for—what?
Betrayal called consumer's right: end user
ceasing use. Exhibit filed with case shut:

You told me as you went. Since then I'm silent
in my searching. Thanks for my betterment.

Je m'appelle

I called you what I'd never called another
woman. You preferred your name, and who
can blame you if you wanted to be other
than generic. But for me my sweetie was you.

Absurd, but when I hear that word in others'
mouths, I look for you, recoil because
it seems they've stolen it, given another
what's yours to have. We dream our private laws.

And if you never call me anymore
what you called me, know that no one does,
its loss a missing *piano* in my ear
until it startles, speaking with my voice.

Ventriloquist, it blurts itself, then scatters.
My nickname's only minims now: three letters.

Floria

Was it here I climbed the willow's fork?
I never fell, but once I lost my balance
where fire built a cone of ash as tall
as a man. Whole hand burnt. It left no mark
except the memory of sudden searing
surprise, the run home and Grandma's rush
to the doctor's, me in tow with wrist clutched
by my other hand and non-stop screaming.

Out of the Roman heat we climbed together
up Castel Sant'Angelo's secret stair
to the end. Great wings and sword, how passion trumped
the villain—until surprising evil met her
with silence. Her stricken shriek still haunts my ear,
like your question: "Could this be where she jumped?"

Après-midi

And so the afternoon has seeped away—
slanting sun, petaled breezes, downy
golden hairs on tan skin, a whiff of Fauré.
Touch gone, gaze on the France of memory.

Yes, there were euphoric hills, and mountains
you could have climbed but didn't dare (so easy
to say). The doubtful gray shade of sun-bleached ruins.
A beach where browning bodies made your throat seize—

and decades later, a man sitting on the ground
in Chartres as you took *ta brune,* who chose you,
through the cathedral's portal and heard a sound
you turned and smiled at—him whistling *La vie en rose.*

And so the afternoon has drifted off—
and touch gone, left only a whiff of Piaf.

The Days Grow Short

And I was left to live what life was left.
I think she thought she'd given me three years
I wouldn't otherwise have had. So where
were thanks? Instead, the wails of one bereft.

Instead, the frantic calls, appeals to deaf
lips. Instead, the searching talks that she
sát through, just to be nice, impatiently.
The ravening nights. The wails of one bereft.

I couldn't face the bedroom, stayed with friends.
Two months to read a map where white despair
marked every compass point, like airless air
beyond the flat earth's rim, a ring of ends.

Memory-plagued, at last I asked the worst.
"I won't forget," she said. "You were my first."

Memories

Memory honors. Does it? Then why say
you must forget what happened to you, not
see again the ceiling slide as you're dropped
to knees by her words, the narrow hallway sways.

Don't re-live the stress, the docs advise.
What of the rest, when every image sends
the reel past years of beauty to The End?
Wipe out self to save it? *Some* compromise.

The science is a fraud. Idyllic islands
under Swedish summer skies can't fail
to raise a hotel window's autumn call.
Beyond the ripping thunder, only silence.

The cure that claims you'll fade them, hardly miss them
is just the same old Terror Management System.

Publisher's Party

"I do PR." "I'm on the marketing team.
My boyfriend's the one who ac'shly reads the books."
"I edit fiction, poetry puzzles me.
It's nice, I guess, but as for sales, it sucks."

"Really? That's my husband's thesis topic."
"Speaker's agent—I book the reading dates."
"My boyfriend says that novel's way erotic."
"We went there in the summer, it was great."

We my boyfriend husband Significant Other.
We my fiancé my legal mate.
We my live-in love or made-up cover
story—Oui, mon cher, you are too late.

I'll play hot and taken, even smart.
You be kindly mentor. Now, talk art.

Encore

Late one night I pulled an early book of yours
and read again in French a story I recalled
from one of those anthologies that Canada
ladders now and then against the lonely wall
between its languages. Your voice your violin
smiling through the dead-end job, the English boss.
Then I turned it over, shocked I had forgotten
that photo of a younger you—and puzzled too

at why I felt I'd known you then, before we met.
We both know why, we know that some connections cancel
pasts endured apart, recover notes half faded
in unredeemed time. And yet, you don't answer
when I write: guarding work or fear, I guess.
Years gone, books high. The link denied. Doubled loss.

VI Bourrée

Hip

Decided to be young and hip forever.
Hip was cool, but youth gave certain trouble,
and those who had it hadn't yet discovered
that ageless hip transcends each trendy bubble.

I'd like to say, Why stumble on a number?
but I'm the only one who'd be persuaded.
Canny shoppers fear the slightest fumble—
Farsighted? Maybe. Also maybe jaded.

The Web of options tents a strange bazaar
with ranked desiderata sought and sold;
before a feeling stirs, a googled year
is churned through Babbage cogs—the sum: Too old.

The game's not looks or talent, sex, romance.
It's youth alone. And then we're maiden aunts.

Left Over

The thirty-year (recovered) alcoholic,
the defrocked priest, the high-school nerd, the lousy
dresser who also suffers halitosis,
the beer-gut former jock, now gray, the boozy

civil servant, boisterous salesman, reformed
embezzler, con man, burglar, arsonist, cheat,
the guy who gets his jollies watching worms
crushed by high heels, the backyard griller of meat,

the death-row killer, gangster on the lam,
the shut-in agoraphobe, the amputee,
the octogenarian widower, a hopeless ham,
and yet other types with no resemblance to me

are pleased to announce their engagement to be wed—
each to a gorgeous woman he finds incred

ible.

Titles

Mister Greenwald, Doctor Greenwald, Sir
are known to merchants from my credit card;
to restaurateurs; to dentists, who prefer
Doctor, knowing such degrees come hard.

Sir's the nameless name from civil clerks,
waiters, tellers, clothing sellers, shills.
Sometimes, if annoyed, it's tinged with snark:
"*Sir!*—I can't, I'm sorry, that's our rules."

But who the hell is Dr. Mister Sir?
He wasn't born so, unlike Mr. Biswas.
An alien has brought these monikers,
an ageing, strangely formal public presence.

To lodge in him and bask in bought respect
doesn't yield, though, the love you'd love to get.

Old Friend

You are the one I tell my days, I tell them
on the keys of a laptop computer and you read
across time we can't count. In silence you read
about music: notes and younger hands that played them.

And you write back, you say your trio met
on Thursday, pondered new pages, dots
as dense as years—in suspended time, the dots
like Morse code for ageing, though when we met

they were long since written, and hadn't changed.
The music always waits—and keeps its figure.
Still fresh when we meet, it'll hear us try to figure
who we are, ask ourselves what's changed.

The future's length has changed. But we're still us.
Just didn't catch it *then;* and deafness filled us.

Find Your Old Classmates

The girl who slipped her thigh between your legs
at a dance in junior high and pressed it up
against your boner, hair an eddied black
spring of heady fragrance, hint of musk

rising from olive skin the color of Sabra,
Greek or Sephardi, Mediterranean pasts;
who learned to light the Sabbath candelabra
while you grew up with cultured communists

—she's on your screen now, all these decades later:
southwestern Jewish Buddhist, stout as a barrel,
no doubt a mom, generous donor, defender
of poor Latinos caught in legal quarrels.

And if asked, "Who's this? from Junior High 143,"
she'd stare, and shrug, and say at last, "Search me!"

Tidal Wave

No, dear friend, *tsunami* isn't Yiddish,
it's English via Japanese. For once
a common error gets corrected, science
pulls the tides away from that huge rush

of water, supplies a term whose strangeness suits
the overwhelming influx we mean. You wonder
how I deal with flooding absence. Longing blots
the years it's drowned in silt, and still we're under

tons of roiling blue-green weight—and a spume
of whitening void that Hokusai couldn't paint.
We can only be silkie or skerry, send up plumes
of breath or foam. The waves don't relent.

Here's my answer, which won't help you much:
When walls of ocean land on me, I'm crushed.

Paused

I am paused halfway up the stairs,
the flight between the second floor and third.
No rail, gray carpet, lean against the wall.
Listen. Listen. Nothing. Is there more?

The only force-field here is from the wires
in the wall. No word from Europe or the hippo-
campus, swampy college of thoughts without
their glasses. I cóuld sit down, but rest assured

that only people expecting to be found
by other actors plop down on steps
for medium shots. The house is dark, the keys
slung in my pocket are the only set.

No playing piano or making meals.
Though I may remember something in a while.

Obits [1]

Why do you want to know how people died?
A vague announcement makes you wonder: Was it
really accidental—or suicide?
"Lengthy illness" signals cancer. Or does it?

How do these case histories avail you?
As if quick twist could let the *toro* pass.
You know in thís, precaution's bound to fail you:
the horn will catch and land you on your ass.

How much longer is your life for scoring
a thousand threats averted? How narrowed
by your caped glissades? It's you that's goring
time in needless swiveling from shadows.

From futile reading, caution's weakness dawns:
It's of forearmed we need to be forewarned.

Facts

O Joel, you shouldn't've left us, not at the age
that's reached me now, imposed its stubborn facts:
injury regret and longing; rage
at fate that won't provide the second act

all Americans hope for, most in vain.
If your rich living drew an early entrance
by the fifth-act killer of your lung and brain,
I've probably got decades to do penance

for loyal loving, vivid grief, bad luck—
the many engines of emptiness we've learned
from comedic doctors must be my constructions,
though blaming the wronged is a wrong they claim to spurn.

Lover, father, poet, man: I know
you're watching this fiasco kindly, Joel.

VII Pavane

At 65

In my dreams my friends are getting younger:
Kern arrives with hair that's short and brown,
Strier's tennis beats Professor Wagner,
Peter Anson picks a banjo tune,

Sloman and Sarita dance like crazy,
Robert David's naked on the stage.
Soon they're teens, then toddlers, even babies;
but then their kids', or now their grandkids', age.

And where am I in this, the gray-haired dreamer
still looking, unresigned, for the main event.
The curvy clouds seem more or less like summer;
but I wake in snow, can't see where summer went.

No wife, no kids or grandkids—yearning pulse;
but in the mirror, pushing eighty, Grandpa's face.

Associations

Why not take a nap this afternoon
in April, with the forecast *winter storm,*
the sky dark gray and blown rain slanting down,
not freezing yet; a villanelle of yawns

nudging you toward the warmth of eiderdown
and rhyming trills on angled roof, a sound
you'd think would conjure up the weeping town
Verlaine sang of—the poem's soothing pain.

But a roof in rainy Bergen comes to mind
instead, a fish you chalked on wooden planks
that sloped above the bed, Pisces on pine,
sign of your love, your overflowing thanks.

Each time you woke, her clear eyes met your gaze.
Their shining shuts out sleep this rainy day.

Report, Much Later

By bike I found a street far west of me,
leaf-lined, that I coasted down in stages.
At bottom open grass and one broad tree
whose shade protected the many resting players.

A baseball game was going on the field,
had drifted into inning sixty-seven,
and no one cared the scoreboard wasn't tied:
the summer sun was set to pitch forever.

And there was Scott, sitting back to tree-trunk,
nineteen, with gray-blue eyes he didn't have.
Looked up at me but clearly didn't know me.
I stood there with my bike and couldn't move.

Hotel machinery, whining, broke my sleep.
Boston, a lifetime later. Snow and sleet.

Filled Time

The things that were a waste of time were most
things. Like chess, Monopoly, Perquacky,
Parchesi, Scrabble, checkers, Hangman, Ghost,
jigsaws, science fiction, watching hockey.

What did these prepare you for, exactly?
Or gluing toothpicks in Construction class,
tracing diagrams by textbook hacks, re-
hearsing Broadway show tunes, fishing bass.

If only sonnets grew from games and glue
and then received as much response as sport
from ardent fans. Is writing poems too
a dodge to fend off want, a paper fort?

I close the gate and try to lock the latch,
but empty time's a match. No, not a mate.

Prometheans

Do we all know where we're at now, guys?
We love to gather: us, our wits, and any
inferences a text can justify.
Three of six are parents, but how many

wanted it? Some things remain unknown,
even as the traits we recognize
exclaim, "Só *him!*" I hope you don't suppose
that unbegotten must mean undesired.

Discreet, we've never said what each of us
has thought: the years will close parentheses,
one of us will be remaindered first.
In sidewalk stalls the reader is the breeze.

Brothers! Rich our past, our gatherings good.
But the future is a threatening neighborhood.

The Finger

This one's bladder, that one's lung—the erasing
finger rubs, and having rubbed, moves on
—not all your poisons or your burning rays
can stave it off one bit. Khayyám's dawn

was noose indeed, its rope now reeling up,
speeding up, skinning hands that won't
get purchase. No tug-of-war when rough
decrees condemn the lost, make struggle moot.

Remember when you watched as time slowed down,
the rubber ball approached the sewer grate,
the seconds ticked, you couldn't move, and how
the drop seemed rendered destined by the wait?

Now time races, space contracts, and grief
knots dusk. You search your life for signs of life.

Obits [2]

I follow science, but the brilliant work
of some experimenters reaches me
only on their deaths. Their sudden spark
of insight, smart design, persistence, savvy—

these move me and impress. The poet envies
how their boldest moves found vindication—
and havens safer than anthologies—
yet cheers their feats with reasoned admiration.

But reading writers' lives is grimly sad:
their celebrations rub my misses in.
The wives, awards, and kids the great man had.
I'm late. Now breathing's all I've got on him.

And it's short: the flapping jacket starts to pinch.
I'll have to pay up for my column inch.

The Ode

A short old Jew was leafing fashion mags
in the newsstand part of a department store.
I figured he must once have worked in rags
and browsed to keep abreast. It was a score

of years ago, but the image stays with me:
the pale *Vogue* models, tall beneath his hands,
a glossy past abroad. And I could see
my future, the fluorescent evil wands

above us droned the tune of men alone.
Und wer's nie gekonnt, der stehle, sang
the Ode of banished joy. Here's a stone
for dinner; here's a tablet for your pangs.

I never made a garment, but rended some
and tore my hair. What came was quick to come.

Syl

Forty years of love, then thirty-five
of mourning. This the life of my most esteemed
aunt, my great-aunt Sylvia. I give
scant space to her teaching, childless woman's scheme

for spreading love around, or to her singing
in all the years after Alvin died,
Doctor Alvin Hollander, whose shining
bald head I spotted from the cheapest heights

of Carnegie Hall, hearing Bach's great Mass
with Scott in college. It became a family joke.
After his war, her choir; to help her rehearse
he took up piano at fifty. At sixty: stroke.

She couldn't think of finding someone else.
Forty years of love; the rest was loss.

3 A.M.

I’m writing poems in my sleep, or almost.
I don’t mean it’s easy. Not at all.
Or that to find my way I need a deep
trance state (which helps). I mean I have to put

my mind to puzzling jobs or else it turns
to flailing in the reservoir of dread.
Better to hunt a rhyme that ends up false
than quiver through the wolf’s corrosive hour.

My grandpa used my stepdad’s Master of Arts
diploma to divide a dresser drawer.
A sturdy piece of cardboard cut in halves.
Can I let Uncle’s framed MD be trash?

He had no kids! I have no kids! My rescue
just delays it. 3 a.m. Dread dread.

Checkmate

When Death enters, he shifts the names of things.
Your oldest friend becomes your boyhood pal;
your New York aunt becomes your late Aunt Syl.
Relatives get ré-named next-of-kin.

He merely shows his shape and memories
convert from startings-out and nervy leaps
to dwindling faces you can barely keep—
to vivid emblems of the unachieved.

How push back? Declare there's time and hope.
Imagine second chances—fantasies
in which some lovely younger friend is seized
by longing to be near you. What a trope.

Language never swayed your leaving love
and won't delay the black lord's pending move.

Whose Name

I know what Death will look like, she will wear
round glasses, false front teeth (a childhood fall);
one thigh will have a darkened oval, a scar
below her lower lip will itch. All

my adult years she's been with me, at first
so close I used my teeth to scratch that scar,
then so far the oval's nebula curled
into a pointlike source, a pulsing star

whose name I won't forget. When almost there
I'll say its sounds, I'll be the only one
who can pronounce it, and whoever hears
will puzzle over how the syllables join.

Can't grasp what sort of Love supplied these lines?
Simple: Death was my Life before she died.

Clouded Isle

My life reeks death, not others', mine:
the stumbled circles on an always clouded
isle, as ferries run sunny channels
that lead somewhere. Fate's a kind of weather,

and *pace* Donne, microclimatic zones
do sever some of us from main and order,
pattern, link, relation, antic light—
or anyway, delay rhyme's arrival

until too late, when picnic plans yield
to panic, maps go blank, and hugging shore,
thick, pearly banks swing low
and make the stuff we breathe gray as the brain.

But I still keep watch for even the palest signs,
pining to sing of moonlight through the fog.

VIII Gigue

Sundays Early

In summer camp on Sundays early, my counselor,
Ed Raditz, Oklahoman Jewish, practiced
violin, his part in Tulsa's orchestra,
and I, thirteen, already night-owl, mastered

my genes to rise with him and listen. The empty
Social Hall rec room, paved in linoleum,
echoed the tinny record player, yet it
sang with wood and strings the Ninth's adagio.

And lanky man and chubby boy grew serious
while hundreds slept and dozens cooked our breakfasts.
Why *this* boy? thought Ed—and I was curious:
could words as well be made to say the wordless?

Ed's the chair of Music at a school out East;
my bookshelves bend under countless CDs.

Emergency

No argument. It's afternoon and M
goes into labor. Call someone! the concert
starts at 8! *Okay, I'll catch a plane,*
be there and changed by 9. Explain. Insert

an overture. She scans the score in transit,
smiles on stage: (Now I'm really winging it!).
The music's airborne, audience ecstatic.
This rescue has a name: Emergency Singing.

> I sat on a hallway chair and rocked, the words
> a frantic lullaby I sang myself
> in a homespun tongue whose speaker would not return
> as I waited for a Pass too late by half.

His baritone beside her chants, then surges.
The infant crowns, follows her ears, emerges.

Kisses

Didn't guess *Bésame mucho*'s in a minor
key. Did I know that kisses can be vin-
egar? Since ancient Greece and Rome they're wine or
honey. Kisses live though lovers have been
and gone. Catullus counts them till he can't
keep track. A song says they remain as time
goes by. In madrigals men die for want
of kisses. Troubadors lament in rhyme

their sweetest unattainability.
Which sours when the cheating Guinevere
and Lancelot demolish fealty.
Now kisses turn when separation's near
so tongue-play dries to pecked civility.
Consuelo's fear of loss invades the ear.

Judgment of the Moon and Stars

In the Opus Hundred-ten sonata
a voice that walks across the stage, soon followed
by other versions of itself, encounters
the paradox of fugue: to be allowed

to lead, or act as if it's leading, then
lose its prominence as others crowd
the space, get louder, circle-dance.
The older voice wishes it could be caught.

And now it pushes at the door, prepares
to break a path to Opus One-eleven,
where it will build a bigger hall and tear it
down, grow heavy wings, and sail to heaven.

It's raised by gravity and can't retreat
to younger selves. Black notes reverberate.

Sara

Soft-voiced Sara between two worlds. The ancient
Abandoned one, removed from time, awaiting
Dissolution of the absolutes.
Exile, a landing where you're free for nothing.

You've entered a concrete orchard of unripe fruits.
English becomes second nature, while Persian
Dreams the past inside its satin-lined suitcase.
Language feeds you; foods unleash aversion.

And I am with you here, though not enough.
Deficits abound for both of us.
You ask how is it basics are so tough—
Others seem to coast to their sun-filled places.

For me your laugh conjures a white-blue cove.
If only—but that rhyme is not to be.

Attuned

A glance, a smile, exchanged across a table.
Maker of verses, intricate or sharp.
Maker of complicated rhythms, rapped
or rubbed, or tapped as metal ringlets tremble.

He can hear them but can't read music. She,
who plays the daf and sings like mountain air,
lives in two tongues and can't tell *pair* from *pear*
or spell the rhyming couples right in Farsi.

And yet one voice fits in the other's ear
and one ear wraps around the other voice.
In this unexpected correspondence
distances converge; far becomes near.

But far is with us. Years can't be redeemed.
Yearning smiles are parted by their slipstream.

Con Sordino

Guests gone, I splashed my face, suddenly wondered
if she'd left her scent on the blue towel, plunged
in—moved in the blueness by my move. No trace.
At times a gesture's all one can speak. Mute hue.

The five of us, my friend, her sister, parents,
and I, the host, had lingered over dinner,
the emigrés not guessing how I strained
with my own foreignness. The chronic sting.

Yet for two seconds, looking up before
she spoke, she saw my silent smile and stopped,
returned it (did sister catch?). Ensconced by books:
in refuge from our refuge for a while.

Some bonds are deeper than eros, even those
you wish in vain would draw the god's arrows.

Casey Sokol's Improv Soirées

For the time being we áre together in time,
being in the music with one another,
where virtual minutes form, form unwinds,
and the ageless space makes us sisters and brothers.

Young Avesta reincarnates Scott,
my lifelong pal, who's gone, yet part of me.
Victoria, Kousha, others Casey's taught;
Mike, Dominique, Celine, and Ann-Marie.

But music ends, each life erodes its path,
you dance or sing, I write, and time, returned
to being age, picks up its fatal math.
Sleep cracks, nerves quake, gut churns, dread images surge.

Some of you will bury me someday.
If you come, just find your groove—and play!

Time

Day dawns. You meet the one whose name you'll say your
whole life (though on another day she will
run off). A distant smile and then she takes your
bus. Change a tick and other coin were milled.

Day breaks. Professor Borg sets out for Lund.
Long dreams, a life precede the honor. Still,
bells toll when tolled. O hear, the day is one,
just one. Old summers fill the later lull.

Earth turns. A village stirs in Vietnam.
Doom revs its blades. Now jellied fire sears
air, flesh. Unmeant, a meteor might land
just so, a moment blotting out all years.

Time's weight is light as ash that almost falls,
then falls. Or not. As sound when nothing calls.

Portals

Although they're gone, still it seems worth saying
these openings to other worlds were not
among the singer's tones, the swaying boats,
or beyond us in the evening's constellations.

They bloomed where we erased the space between us,
shrank distances so closeness sailed us far:
our nerves forgot where skin's old boundaries were,
the astrocytes were stargates deep within us.

Gone, because we drift, close up again.
Or óne does—frightens, pales, contracts, retreats.
A body only body is not sweet;
after love, mere pairing's dim with pain.

And yet with luck we can, before we're barred,
pass through fragrant portals, brightly starred.

Song of Songs

Compose yourself for leaving. Take this moment
in the garden. Stillness. Only bees moving.
Full, or empty? What's "empty" but tormented
fullness? Leafy absence, calm unloving

reminders that potential's failed. The oak
and aspen, birches, pines, the bluish spruce
embraced you once, now mock the ghostly yoke
that joins to nothing. Leaves are hanging loose

as yóu fall by rote to reverie.
Bags packed, you wait. The prospect dims because
the cumulating past lacks energy.
A person at rest alone has only pause

in which to note the garden's sunny calm:
in which to wish the grounds were there for psalm.

Keener Sounds

Can feelings freed of words set people free?
Or, is music's promise false salvation?
A dream more vain: that notes unheard are sweeter.
Voice is the source of every transformation.

Does form redeem, then? beauty help? or passion?
Perhaps—if tones and rhythms slowly weave
their colors through the words' recurring pattern,
always new yet recognized forever.

The sacred shadows hold a double lesson:
death comes first, heaven only later.
No wonder there's a plaintive exultation
that stabs me in Charpentier's steady quaver.

Here's the mark of art that cleanses wounds:
embodied words, entwined in keener sounds.

Notes

The poems were written over an extended period and are not presented in chronological order.

Aubade *p. 15*

For HA, Izmir.

Handan: A woman's first name in Turkish.

Prélude

Annbjørg Lien *p. 22*

"Rosa" [The Rose] is one of the most famous traditional melodies from Telemark. Annbjørg Lien has issued a live concert recording of her extraordinary version of it, played solo on the Hardanger fiddle, on her CD *Aliens Alive* (Grappa GRCD 4178, or in the U.S., NorthSide NSD 6068).

Bridal March *p. 23*

Beiarn: a municipal region in northern Norway, in Nordland County. The *brudemarsj* in question is by Johan A. Aronsen (1876–1965) and can be heard on Susanne Lundeng's CD *Havella: Slåtter fra Nordland* (Heilo HCD 7067) and in an arranged version on her CD *Drag* (Kirkelig Kulturverksted-Aschehoug FXCD 140-1994). *Brudemarsj* is often translated as "wedding march."

Ethos and Mythos *p. 24*

The Body's Rapture: the title of the English translation by John Rodker of a novel by Jules Romains published in French in three parts in 1933 under the general title *Psyché.*

Happiness *p. 25*

For GE.

Danmarks Plass: a small plaza next to a heavily trafficked roadway, not in Denmark.

Busserull: a collarless over-the-head shirt of heavy cotton, blue or red with thin white stripes, originally worn by the laborers who built Norway's railroads.

Halfway There *p. 31*

"Somewhere," from *West Side Story,* music by Leonard Bernstein (with a debt, in this song, to Beethoven), lyrics by Stephen Sondheim.

Remembrance *p. 32*

"the lazy crescent river": the Shark River, at Shark River Hills, New Jersey.

Numbers *p. 33*

Radar signals were first reflected off the moon and received back on Earth on 10 January 1946 (Project Diana) by a team of scientists under the direction of Lt. Col. John J. DeWitt at the Belmar, New Jersey, site of the Evans Signal Laboratory, which was operated by the U.S. Army's Signal Corps Laboratories based in Fort Monmouth, New Jersey (*A history of Army communications and electronics at Fort Monmouth, New Jersey, 1917–2007,* Chapter 4, p. 29, https://archive.org/details/historyofarmycom00fort.pdf [accessed 17 Jan. 2025]).

Phoenix *p. 34*

Gedalyah Halpern (1891–1979).

"Gey gezunterheyt": Go in good health.

Forverts: the Yiddish newspaper known in English as *The Jewish Daily Forward,* where for most of his life G. Halpern worked as a Linotype operator.

Night *p. 37*

The last sentence is adapted from Kafka: "die Nacht ist noch zu wenig Nacht" (letter to Felice Bauer, 14–15 January 1913, in *Briefe an Felice und andere Korrespondenz aus der Verlobungszeit,* ed. Erich Heller and Jörgen Born [New York: S. Fischer Verlag/Schocken Books, 1967], 250).

The Word *Wife*   *p. 39*

The Nights of Summer: Berlioz, *Les nuits d'été,* to poems by Théophile Gautier. (The omission of quotation marks and italics in the sestet is intentional.)

Mettle   *p. 40*

"the love bit": Joel Oppenheimer, *The Love Bit, and Other Poems* (New York: Totem Press / Corinth Books, 1962).

Courante

Sightseeing   *p. 45*

Munkholmen (called Nidarholm until 1537): a small island in the Trondheim Fjord, just outside of Trondheim; site of a cloister founded in the early 1100s or possibly as early as 1028 and active until 1537; after 1660, site of a fortress, ruins of which remain. *Munk* means monk; *holm* means small island.

Sarabande

The Deep Heart's Core   *p. 55*

Sylvia Jean Halpern (1919–2005); Lewis Greenwald (1918–1948).

Cancer   *p. 56*

"We want you to be prepared to respond in ways that will help your loved one accomplish this transition with support, understanding and ease.... We are here to walk the journey with you..." (*A Very Special Journey* [West Palm Beach, Florida: Hospice of Palm Beach County, 2003]).

New Year's Eve   *p. 61*

"drops the ball": "The Times Square Ball is a time ball that has been lowered or 'dropped' from the flagpole of One Times Square nearly every New Year's Eve since December 31, 1907 in Times Square, Manhattan, New York City. The ball (now in its sixth incarnation) is currently made by Waterford Crystal. Since 2009, the ball remains on the flagpole over One Times Square year-round, and is only lowered on New Year's Eve or removed for general maintenance. Every December 31 at 11:59 p.m. EST, the ball descends 77 feet (23 m) over the course of a minute, coming to rest at the bottom of the flagpole at midnight, where a sign lights up with the digits of the new year, as the ball's lights turn off at the same time." —Wikipedia (17 Jan. 2012)

Grandpa Charlie: Charles Kalman Greenwald (1879–1968).

Nana: Marie Hollander Greenwald (ca. 1893–1961).

Sunday Nights *p. 63*

SSRIs: selective serotonin reuptake inhibitors, a class of antidepressant drugs.

Gavotte

Je m'appelle *p. 71*

For CZ.

Floria *p. 72*

Floria Tosca.

"Great wings and sword": see the bronze statue of the archangel Michael that stands atop the Castel Sant'Angelo, modelled in 1753 by Peter Anton von Verschaffelt (1710–1793).

The Days Grow Short *p. 74*

With a nod to Kurt Weill and Maxwell Anderson ("September Song").

Memories *p. 75*

"Terror Management System": a theory about the evolution in humans of psychological mechanisms to cope with the fear of death.

Encore *p. 77*

In memory of DS, who did reply after a while.

Bourrée

Titles *p. 85*

"Mr. Biswas": The main character in *A House for Mr Biswas,* by V. S. Naipaul, is referred to by the narrator as "Mr" even when he is a child.

Find Your Old Classmates *p. 87*

The title was a frequent header or subject line in unsolicited ads for search services when the Internet was beginning to reach a large population.

"Search me!": a colloquial phrase once common in New York City, meaning "I have no idea!" (That is, the communicated sense, "Don't ask me," is the opposite of the literal sense, "Ask me.")

Tidal Wave *p. 88*

This poem was written in August, 2004, four months before the catastrophic tsunami of December 26th struck countries with coastlines on the Indian Ocean and adjoining bodies of water.

Facts *p. 91*

Joel Oppenheimer, American poet (1930–1988).

Pavane

Report, Much Later *p. 99*

Cf. "Report" in *Connecting Flight.*

Prometheans *p. 101*

Promethean was and is the literary magazine of the City College of New York. The title refers to a group of six alumni who in the 1960s edited or contributed to the magazine and participated in its weekly writers' workshops. Cf. "At 65."

The Finger *p. 102*

See the first edition of Edward FitzGerald's translation of the *Rubáiyát of Omar Khayyám.*

The Ode *p. 104*

Schiller's "An die Freude," or Beethoven's Ninth:

Wem der grosse Wurf gelungen,
Eines Freundes Freund zu sein,
Wer ein holdes Weib errungen,
Mische seinen Jubel ein!
Ja—wer auch nur eine Seele
Sein nennt auf dem Erdenrund!
Und wer's nie gekonnt, der stehle
Weinend sich aus diesem Bund.

Whoever has the great good fortune
To be friends with friends who trust,
Whoever's wed a precious woman,
Let him celebrate with us!
Yes—whoever calls a single
Soul his own in all the world!
And whoever can't goes slinking,
Tearfully, from our guild. [RG]

Syl *p. 105*

Sylvia Sonnenblick Hollander (1914–2011), an elementary school teacher and a longtime soprano member of the New York Oratorio Society.

Alvin Hollander (1912–1974), a veteran of World War II (Pacific theater) and a skilled and compassionate practitioner of the art of medicine.

Checkmate *p. 107*

"the black lord": See Ingmar Bergman, *Det sjunde inseglet (The Seventh Seal).*

Clouded Isle *p. 109*

With a nod to Hoagy Carmichael and Stuart Gorrell ("Georgia on My Mind").

Gigue

Kisses *p. 117*

"Bésame mucho" was written in Mexico by Consuelo Velázquez in 1940. As published, it was in C minor.

Judgment of the Moon and Stars *p. 118*

The title refers to Joni Mitchell's song "Judgement of the Moon and Stars (Ludwig's Tune)," from her 1972 album, *For the Roses.*

Sara *p. 119*

"a landing": In addition to its usual meanings, "landing" refers to the process by which a person becomes a "landed immigrant" in Canada: one with permanent residence and the right to work and to apply for citizenship after a fixed number of years.

"free for nothing": a phrase from Jean-Paul Sartre's 1945 novel *Le sursis (The Reprieve),* in which Mathieu reflects, "Je suis libre pour rien" (268).

Attuned *p. 120*

"plays the daf": A daf (or dap) is a large Persian frame drum that has metal ringlets attached to the frame.

Con Sordino *p. 121*

Title: "with the mute" (a direction to musicians).

"the god's arrows": Cupid's.

Casey Sokol's Improv Soirées *p. 122*

Casey Sokol: American-Canadian pianist, improviser, and composer. Professor of Music at York University, Toronto.

Time *p. 123*

Professor Borg: Ingmar Bergman, *Smultronstället (Wild Strawberries).*

Vietnam: Francis Ford Coppola, *Apocalypse Now.*

Keener Sounds p. 127

Marc-Antoine Charpentier (1645–1704), the greatest composer of the French Baroque period.

Acknowledgments

My thanks to all those who have read and offered comments on poems and on various drafts of this book, including Peter Anson, Aliki Barnstone, Luigi M. Bianchi, Barry Callaghan, Robert David Cohen, Charles Douglas, Daryl Fridenberg, Karl Kirchwey, Richard M. Lush, Anne Michaels, Francine Sterle, Richard Strier, Richard Teleky, Monika van Paemel, Robert von Hallberg, Rosanna Warren, and David Wevill. Special thanks to Glenna Munro for expert advice.

— RG

The following journals published the listed poems:

Exile Magazine (Gwendolyn MacEwen Poetry Award): "Aubade," "Auditorium," "Annbjørg Lien," "Ethos and Mythos," "Syl," "Song of Songs"

Stand Magazine: "Night," "Kisses"

ROGER GREENWALD attended The City College of New York and the Poetry Project workshop at St. Mark's Church In-the-Bowery, then completed graduate degrees at the University of Toronto. He has won two CBC Literary Awards, the Gwendolyn MacEwen Poetry Award, the Littoral Press Poetry Prize, and many awards for translations from Scandinavian languages. He has published four earlier books of poems: *Connecting Flight, Slow Mountain Train, The Half-Life,* and *An Opening in the Vertical World.*

ARIELLE SANDLER holds a BFA in painting from Washington University in St. Louis. Her paintings have appeared in movies, television programs, and publications including *The New York Times* and *New American Paintings.* Her work is in museum, corporate, public, and private collections around the world.

BLACK WIDOW PRESS :: POETRY IN TRANSLATION

Approximate Man and Other Writings by Tristan Tzara. Translated and edited by Mary Ann Caws.

Art Poétique by Guillevic. Translated by Maureen Smith.

Beginnings of the Prose Poem. Edited by Mary Ann Caws, Michel Delville.

The Big Game by Benjamin Péret. Translated with an introduction by Marilyn Kallet.

Boris Vian Invents Boris Vian: A Boris Vian Reader. Edited and translated by Julia Older.

Capital of Pain by Paul Eluard. Translated by Mary Ann Caws, Patricia Terry, and Nancy Kline.

Chanson Dada: Selected Poems by Tristan Tzara. Translated with an introduction and essay by Lee Harwood.

Earthlight (Clair de Terre) by André Breton. Translated by Bill Zavatsky and Zack Rogow. (New and revised edition.)

Essential Poems and Prose of Jules Laforgue. Translated and edited by Patricia Terry.

Essential Poems and Writings of Joyce Mansour: A Bilingual Anthology. Translated with an introduction by Serge Gavronsky.

Essential Poems and Writings of Robert Desnos: A Bilingual Anthology. Edited with introduction & essay by Mary Ann Caws.

EyeSeas (Les Ziaux) by Raymond Queneau. Translated with an introduction by Daniela Hurezanu and Stephen Kessler.

Fables in a Modern Key by Pierre Coran. Translated by Norman R. Shapiro. Full-color illustrations by Olga Pastuchiv.

Fables of Town & Country by Pierre Coran. Translated by Norman R. Shapiro. Full-color illustrations by Olga Pastuchiv.

A Flea the Size of Paris: The Old French Fatrasies & Fatras. Edited and translated by Ted Byrne and Donato Mancini.

Forbidden Pleasures: New Selected Poems 1924–1949 by Luis Cernuda. Translated by Stephen Kessler.

Furor and Mystery & Other Writings by René Char. Translated by Mary Ann Caws and Nancy Kline.

The Gentle Genius of Cécile Périn: Selected Poems (1906–1956). Edited & translated by Norman R. Shapiro.

The Great Madness by Avigdor Hameiri. Translated and edited by Peter C. Appelbaum with an introduction by Dan Hecht.

Guarding the Air: Selected Poems of Gunnar Harding. Translated and edited by Roger Greenwald.

Howls & Growls: French Poems to Bark By. Translated by Norman R. Shapiro; illustrated by Olga K. Pastuchiv.

I Have Invented Nothing: Selected Poems by Jean-Pierre Rosnay. Translated by J. Kates.

In Praise of Sleep: Selected Poems of Lucian Blaga. Translated with an introduction by Andrei Codrescu.

The Inventor of Love & Other Writings by Gherasim Luca. Translated by Julian & Laura Semilian. Introduction by Andrei Codrescu. Essay by Petre Răileanu.

Jules Supervielle: Selected Prose and Poetry. Translated by Nancy Kline and Patricia Terry.

La Fontaine's Bawdy by Jean de La Fontaine. Translated with an introduction by Norman R. Shapiro.

Last Love Poems of Paul Eluard. Translated with an introduction by Marilyn Kallet.

A Life of Poems, Poems of a Life by Anna de Noailles. Edited and translated by Norman R. Shapiro. Introduction by Catherine Perry.

Love, Poetry (L'amour la poésie)
by Paul Eluard. Translated with an essay by Stuart Kendall.

Of Human Carnage—Odessa 1918–1920
by Avigdor Hameiri. Translated and edited by Peter C. Appelbaum with an introduction by Dan Hecht.

Pierre Reverdy: Poems, Early to Late.
Translated by Mary Ann Caws and Patricia Terry.

Poems of André Breton: A Bilingual Anthology. Translated with essays by Jean-Pierre Cauvin and Mary Ann Caws.

Poems of A.O. Barnabooth
by Valery Larbaud. Translated by Ron Padgett and Bill Zavatsky.

Poems of Consummation
by Vicente Aleixandre.
Translated by Stephen Kessler.

Préversities: A Jacques Prévert Sampler.
Translated & edited by Norman R. Shapiro.

RhymAmusings (AmuseRimes)
by Pierre Coran. Translated by Norman R. Shapiro.

The Sea and Other Poems
by Guillevic. Translated by Patricia Terry.
Introduction by Monique Chefdor.

Sixty Years: Selected Poems 1957–2017
by Mikhail Yeryomin. Translated by J. Kates.

Through Naked Branches
by Tarjei Vesaas. Translated, edited, and introduced by Roger Greenwald.

To Speak, to Tell You?
Poems by Sabine Sicaud. Translated by Norman R. Shapiro. Introduction, notes by Odile Ayral-Clause.

The Water Drinkers and Other Sketches of Paris in the Romantic Era
by Henry Murger. Translated and adapted by Zack Rogow.

:: MODERN POETRY SERIES

RALPH ADAMO
All the Good Hiding Places: Poems

WILLIS BARNSTONE
ABC of Translation
African Bestiary (Forthcoming)

DAVE BRINKS
The Caveat Onus
The Secret Brain: Selected Poems 1995–2012

RUXANDRA CESEREANU
California (on the Someș)
Translated with Adam J. Sorkin.
Crusader-Woman
Translated by Adam J. Sorkin;
Introduction by Andrei Codrescu.
Forgiven Submarine
with Andrei Codrescu.

ANDREI CODRESCU
A Possible Epic of Care, with Vincent Katz
Forgiven Submarine,
with Ruxandra Cesereanu
How to Live Under Fascism (Forthcoming)
Too Late for Nightmares: Poems

CLAYTON ESHLEMAN
An Alchemist with One Eye on Fire
Anticline
Archaic Design
The Essential Poetry: 1960–2015
Grindstone of Rapport: A Clayton Eshleman Reader
Penetralia
Pollen Aria
The Price of Experience
Endure: Poems by Bei Dao. Translated with Lucas Klein.
Curdled Skulls: Poems of Bernard Bador.
Translated with Bernard Bador.

ROGER GREENWALD
An Opening in the Vertical World
Keener Sounds: A Suite

PIERRE JORIS
Barzakh (Poems 2000–2012)
Exile Is My Trade: A Habib Tengour Reader

...

MARILYN KALLET
Even When We Sleep
How Our Bodies Learned
Packing Light: New and Selected Poems
The Love That Moves Me
Disenchanted City (La ville désenchantée)
by Chantal Bizzini. Translated by J. Bradford Anderson, Darren Jackson, and Marilyn Kallet.

ROBERT KELLY
Fire Exit
The Hexagon

STEPHEN KESSLER
Garage Elegies
Last Call

BILL LAVENDER
Memory Wing

HELLER LEVINSON
Crossfall (Forthcoming)
from stone this running
jus' sayn'
LinguaQuake
Lure
Lurk
Query Caboodle
Seep
Shift Gristle
Tenebraed
Un-
Valvular Ash
Wrack Lariat

JOHN OLSON
Backscatter: New and Selected Poems
Dada Budapest
Larynx Galaxy
Weave of the Dream King

NIYI OSUNDARE
City Without People: The Katrina Poems
Green: Sighs of Our Ailing Planet: Poems

MEBANE ROBERTSON
An American Unconscious
Signal from Draco: New and Selected Poems

JEROME ROTHENBERG
Concealments and Caprichos
Eye of Witness: A Jerome Rothenberg Reader
Edited with commentaries by Heriberto Yepez & Jerome Rothenberg.
The President of Desolation & Other Poems

AMINA SAÏD
The Present Tense of the World: Poems 2000–2009
Translated with an introduction by Marilyn Hacker.

JULIAN SEMILIAN
Osiris with a trombone across the seam of insubstance

ANIS SHIVANI
Soraya (Sonnets)

JERRY W. WARD, JR.
Fractal Song

:: ANTHOLOGIES / BIOGRAPHIES

Barbaric Vast & Wild: A Gathering of Outside and Subterranean Poetry (Poems for the Millennium, vol. 5)
Jerome Rothenberg and John Bloomberg-Rissman, eds.

Clayton Eshleman: The Whole Art
by Stuart Kendall

Revolution of the Mind: The Life of André Breton
by Mark Polizzotti